INVESTIGATING
Conspiracy Theories

Fake Birds, Flat Earth,

AND MORE **CONSPIRACY THEORIES**

ABOUT **OUR PLANET**

by Phillip Simpson

CAPSTONE PRESS
a capstone imprint

Published by Captivate, an imprint of Capstone
1710 Roe Crest Drive, North Mankato, Minnesota 56003
capstonepub.com

Library of Congress Cataloging-in-Publication Data is available on the Library of Congress website.
ISBN: 9781669077480 (hardcover)
ISBN: 9781669077435 (paperback)
ISBN: 9781669077442 (ebook PDF)

Summary: Could Earth be flat? Are the birds you see actually robots designed to spy on people? Could giant sharks called megalodons be hunting in the dark depths of the oceans? Some people believe in conspiracy theories about the planet we call home. Take a deep dive into some of these conspiracy theories to discover how they started, why people believe them, and what scientists have to say. Will these conspiracy theories be debunked, or will questions linger?

Editorial Credits
Editor: Carrie Sheely; Designer: Jaime Willems; Media Researcher: Svetlana Zhurkin; Production Specialist: Whitney Schaefer

Image Credits
Alamy: Historic Illustrations, 27, Science History Images, 11; Capstone: Jaime Willems (doodles), cover, back cover, and throughout, Jon Hughes, 19; Getty Images: Bill Wight CA, 15, Manuel Romaris, 10, martinwimmer, 9, Richard I'Anson, 16, ThePalmer, 23; NASA: 12, Goddard Space Flight Center, 26 (right); NOAA: 24; Shutterstock: Aerial-motion, 4, Antonio Viesa, 20, Bestweb, 6, clarst5, 17, cunaplus, 5, Dmitry Vereshchagin (radio antenna and knob), cover, back cover, 1, FotoHelin, 8, Ground Picture, 7, Here Now, 14, Mark_Kostich, 21, Mega Pixel (yellow paper), cover, back cover, and throughout, M-Production, cover (map), Nikolay Suchkov (color pins), cover, back cover, and throughout, Oscar Collica, 22, 26 (left), pics five (string and crumpled paper), cover, back cover, and throughout, Simon J Beer (pigeon), cover, back cover, 1, Skylines (instant photo), 10 and throughout, Steppeland, 13, Tatiana Popova, 29; USGS: M. Patrick, 28

Printed and bound in China. PO 5827

TABLE OF CONTENTS

Chapter 1
What Are Conspiracy Theories? 4

Chapter 2
Flat Earth 8

Chapter 3
Fake Birds 14

Chapter 4
Megalodons Still Exist 18

Chapter 5
Hollow Earth 22

Glossary 30
Read More 31
Internet Sites.. 31
Index 32
About the Author..32

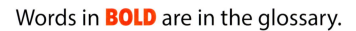

Words in **BOLD** are in the glossary.

Chapter 1

An airplane leaves contrails behind.

WHAT ARE CONSPIRACY THEORIES?

Look up into the sky. Do you see white lines trailing behind an airplane? Could they be chemicals being sprayed purposely to harm the people below? Some people think so! Believers in this conspiracy theory call the trails "chemtrails." They say the white lines are not condensation trails, or contrails, from airplane engine **exhaust**. Instead, they say the trails are harmful chemicals being sprayed by the government or other organizations. They say that normal contrails disappear in a few seconds or minutes. But if it takes longer, it must be a chemtrail.

The contrails chemical conspiracy theory started gaining popularity in the 1990s. At first, people thought a poisonous metal was being sprayed. Today, people believe it could be any of several dangerous chemicals.

Could there be any truth to the chemtrails theory? No. This theory has been proven false. All scientific tests on contrails have shown only normal chemicals in airplane exhaust. Contrails are made when ice particles form in the engine exhaust. This happens in Earth's upper **atmosphere**. Contrails can stay in the sky for many hours.

Fact

Sometimes people confuse contrails with other things in the sky. Smoke or clouds can look like contrails.

SECRET PLOTS

Conspiracy theory believers often say certain events are the result of plots being carried out in secret. They often believe the government or other organizations are involved. Believers in a conspiracy theory usually think that these groups do not have people's best interests at heart. Conspiracy theories reject accepted explanations and **evidence**.

Believing in conspiracy theories and questioning the actions of others is quite common. We don't always want to trust people and events happening around us. According to a study by university researchers, about half of Americans believe at least one conspiracy theory.

Some conspiracy theories involve Earth. They can relate to the makeup of the planet, animals, or everyday happenings. Let's investigate fascinating and outrageous conspiracy theories about the place we call home!

Questions to Ask About Conspiracy Theories

When you find out about a conspiracy theory, do research. Learn as much as you can. It's important not to assume a conspiracy theory is true. Many conspiracy theories can be proven false. For others, parts of them may be true.

- What evidence supports this theory? Ask if there are reliable sources or scientific studies that provide evidence for the claims.
- Who is saying this? What are the sources of information? Consider whether the sources are trustworthy.
- Are there other explanations? Consider different viewpoints. Think critically and weigh different possibilities.
- Has this theory been widely accepted or rejected by experts? Understand the value of expert opinions and scientific evidence. Theories that are widely accepted by experts are generally more reliable than those supported by a few individuals or groups.

Chapter 2

FLAT EARTH

You've learned Earth is round. It might seem like common knowledge. But some people believe in a conspiracy theory called the flat-Earth theory. They think that Earth is not a round ball or **sphere**, but flat like a pancake. People who believe in this theory are called flat-earthers.

IT'S FLAT

Rather than Earth **orbiting** the sun, flat-earthers believe that the sun travels around in a circle above us. They use various claims to try to prove that Earth is flat. They say planes fly straight and level as they travel. Some people say Antarctica makes a wall around the flat Earth. Some flat-earthers think **gravity** works differently from how modern scientists explain it. Some even say gravity doesn't exist.

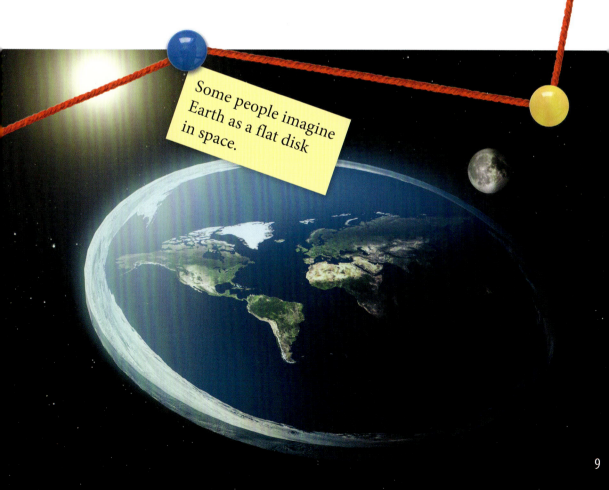

Some people imagine Earth as a flat disk in space.

WHAT SCIENTISTS SAY

The flat-Earth theory has been proven false by existing scientific evidence and knowledge. Pilots don't really fly in straight lines. They account for Earth's curve. They do not need to dip the nose of a plane down. Photos of Antarctica show it does not extend around Earth. The ice wall has been disproved because many explorers have traveled across Antarctica. They didn't find the edge of the world. Scientists have tested and proven the theory of gravity for hundreds of years.

Today, people visit Antarctica as tourists and to do research.

Researchers also point out other evidence that disproves the flat-Earth theory. The sun's gravity keeps Earth in orbit around it. If Earth was flat, scientific knowledge suggests it wouldn't last long. Gravity would quickly turn the planet back into a sphere because it pulls equally from all sides.

A Long-Held Belief

Long ago, most people believed Earth was flat. Some believed that if you reached the edge of the world, you would fall off into a bottomless pit. Others thought that you would be eaten by sea monsters! More than 2,000 years ago, ancient Greeks were some of the first people to understand that Earth isn't flat.

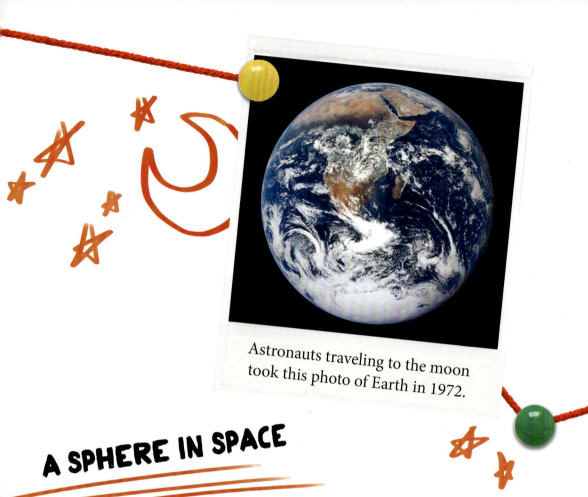

Astronauts traveling to the moon took this photo of Earth in 1972.

A SPHERE IN SPACE

Astronauts have taken pictures from space showing that Earth is a sphere and not flat. In 1930, the first photo showing Earth's curve was taken. Since then, many more images have been taken.

Scientists also use the night sky to disprove the claim that Earth is flat. When you look at stars, you can see only certain stars depending on your location on Earth. For example, people cannot see the star Polaris from the southern half of Earth.

Earth casts its shadow on the moon during a lunar eclipse.

One of the many ways scientists have proven that Earth is round is by studying shadows. For example, during a lunar **eclipse**, Earth casts a round shadow on the moon. This would not be possible if Earth was flat.

Fact

Polaris is also called the North Star. It sits above the North Pole. People use it to find the northern direction.

Chapter 3

FAKE BIRDS

In 2017, graffiti in Memphis, Tennessee, appeared that said, "Birds aren't real." The next year, billboards and posters with the same phrase were seen. What did it mean?

Some people believe in the fake birds conspiracy theory. They think that some of the birds we see outside are not real birds. Instead, they believe the birds are robots or drones created by the government to spy on us.

A Birds Aren't Real rally took place in New York City in 2022.

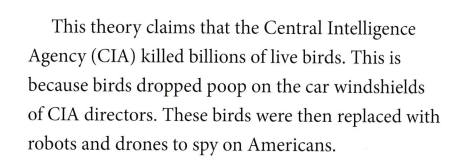

This theory claims that the Central Intelligence Agency (CIA) killed billions of live birds. This is because birds dropped poop on the car windshields of CIA directors. These birds were then replaced with robots and drones to spy on Americans.

Conspiracy theorists say that the government-controlled bird drones use power lines to charge.

THEY'RE REAL, REALLY!

The fake birds theory has been disproven by a large amount of scientific evidence. It shows that birds we see are real living creatures. For example, scientists who study birds note that birds move in unpredictable ways. If birds were drones, they would move in more predictable ways.

Scientists believe birds **evolved** from dinosaurs. They have been around for millions of years. Some are naturally very intelligent. They show this intelligence in different ways. Robots can do only what they are programmed to do.

Fact

The fake birds theory was made up by those who were tired of conspiracy theories. They made it up to prove how easily disinformation and fake news can spread.

Chapter 4

MEGALODONS STILL EXIST

Crunch! A shark as long as a six-story building attacks a whale. In just a few bites, the megalodon finishes its super-sized meal. Could this scene be happening in the oceans today? Some people believe so. Megalodons were the biggest sharks that ever existed. They were much bigger than any modern sharks. However, scientists believe megalodons are **extinct**.

Artwork of a megalodon chasing a sperm whale

The megalodon conspiracy theory suggests that some megalodons have somehow survived extinction. Some believers think that megalodons are living in the deepest unexplored parts of the oceans. This theory cannot be completely disproven because many of the deepest parts of the oceans have not been fully explored.

UNLIKELY ODDS

It's exciting to think that such a massive and fearsome creature still exists. But there is no scientific evidence to support the theory. Scientists have studied the **fossils** and remains of megalodons. They have found that the sharks became extinct about 2.5 to 3 million years ago. A megalodon tooth less than 3.5 million years old has never been found. Sharks lose their teeth throughout their lives. Not finding teeth from more recent times is good evidence that they have died out.

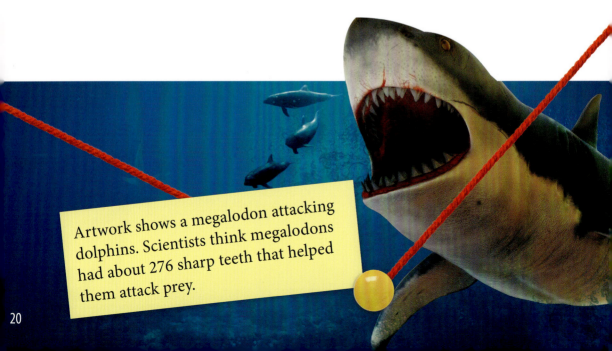

Artwork shows a megalodon attacking dolphins. Scientists think megalodons had about 276 sharp teeth that helped them attack prey.

Scientists think megalodons were up to 60 feet (18 meters) long. Megalodons had rows of sharp teeth that were longer than an adult's hand.

Scientists claim that if megalodons were still alive, they would know about it. This is because megalodons would leave bite marks on other large animals such as whales. Their huge teeth would be found on the ocean floor in great numbers. These sharks often swam in warm coastal waters. If they still existed, it's likely people would easily spot them. It is highly unlikely—although not impossible—that there are living megalodons today.

Chapter 5

HOLLOW EARTH

Giant animals roam through a thick forest. A large, advanced civilization lives alongside the animals. Where are they? Inside Earth!

The hollow-Earth conspiracy theory suggests that Earth is not a solid sphere. Instead, it has a hollow interior with another world or civilizations inside it. A thick shell surrounds the interior.

Hollow-Earth conspiracy theory believers think a shell surrounding Earth's core could be hundreds of miles thick.

Edmond Halley was one of the first scientists to suggest the theory of a hollow Earth. He wrote an article about the theory in 1692. He noticed that Earth's **magnetic field** is unpredictable. He thought this might be because Earth is hollow. Halley thought people lived on the outermost shell and that there could be three more shells inside the planet. He thought the poles of the inner shells affected the magnetic field.

According to this theory, there are secret entrances to the hidden world. These entrances include tunnels or holes at the North and South Poles or in remote places on Earth's surface. The government is covering up proof these entrances exist.

Edmond Halley

Fact

The famous Halley's comet is named after Edmond Halley. He studied the comet and predicted when it would be seen next.

IMAGE QUESTIONS

Believers in the hollow-Earth theory say that some **satellite** images have the poles removed, blurred, or covered. The photos hide the entrances. But scientists explain that satellites don't take pictures of places like the poles very often. This is because little of interest takes place there. However, many satellite images do show the North and South Poles in great detail.

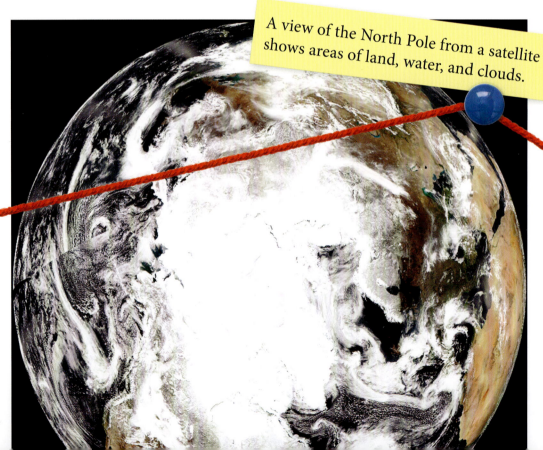

A view of the North Pole from a satellite shows areas of land, water, and clouds.

SCORCHING HOT

Scientists also know that Earth isn't hollow because of earthquakes. Earthquakes produce waves as they move through Earth's interior. The waves appear on scanners, revealing what Earth looks like on the inside.

Scans show the planet's interior is made of layers of different materials. These include the inner core and a liquid outer core. Both cores are very hot. Temperatures can reach 9,000 degrees Fahrenheit (5,000 degrees Celsius). Scientists say that pressure and heat inside Earth make the idea of humans living inside it impossible. In addition, if Earth was hollow, the planet would be much lighter. Gravity would then be much weaker—so weak that we might all float away!

A DEADLY SUN

Believers in the hollow-Earth theory think there might be an inner sun or a different environment inside Earth. If a sun did exist there, it would have to be much smaller than our sun. Our sun is 109 times wider than Earth. Scientists believe that for a sun to fit inside Earth, it would have to be a **neutron star**. The neutron star would have billions of times more gravity than Earth. It would also be filled with deadly **radiation** that would kill all life on the planet!

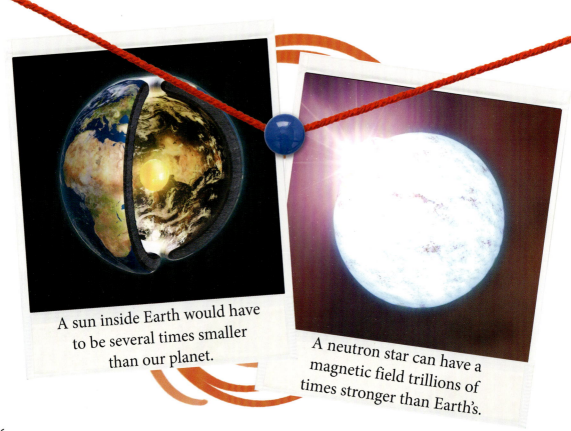

A sun inside Earth would have to be several times smaller than our planet.

A neutron star can have a magnetic field trillions of times stronger than Earth's.

A scene from *Journey to the Center of the Earth*

A Tale to a Conspiracy Theory

The hollow-Earth theory became more popular after the 1864 classic science fiction novel *Journey to the Center of the Earth* was published. In the book, the characters go on a thrilling adventure. They find an entrance to the hollow Earth through a volcanic crater. Inside, they discover a hidden world filled with prehistoric creatures.

ONGOING STUDY

A scientist studies a crater in Kilauea volcano in Hawaii.

Scientists continue to study Earth. They discover new information about its structure, history, and the living creatures on it. They use evidence, research, and observation to understand how Earth works. The work of these scientists is reliable. It is usually able to disprove a conspiracy theory.

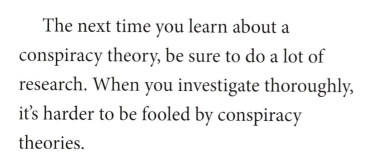

The next time you learn about a conspiracy theory, be sure to do a lot of research. When you investigate thoroughly, it's harder to be fooled by conspiracy theories.

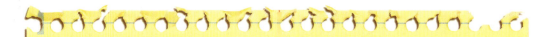

Glossary

atmosphere (AT-muh-sfeer)—the layer of gases that surrounds some planets and moons

eclipse (i-KLIPS)—an event in which Earth's shadow passes over the moon or the moon's shadow passes over Earth

extinct (ik-STINGKT)—no longer living; an extinct animal is one that has died out, with no more of its kind

evidence (EV-uh-duhnss)—information, items, and facts that help prove something to be true or false

evolve (i-VAHLV)—to change gradually over a long time period

exhaust (eg-ZAWST)—the waste gases produced by an engine

fossil (FAH-suhl)—the remains or traces of plants and animals that are preserved as rock

gravity (GRAV-uh-tee)—a force that pulls objects with mass together

magnetic field (mag-NET-ik FEELD)—the space near a magnetic body or current-carrying body in which magnetic forces can be detected

neutron star (NOO-trahn STAR)—the dense, caved-in core of a star that has exploded

orbit (OR-bit)—to travel around an object in space

radiation (ray-dee-AY-shuhn)—rays of energy given off by certain elements

satellite (SAT-uh-lite)—a spacecraft used to send signals and information from one place to another

sphere (SFEER)—a round object

Read More

Goldstein, Margaret J. *What Are Conspiracy Theories?* Minneapolis: Lerner Publications, 2020.

Gravel, Elise. *Killer Underwear Invasion!: How to Spot Fake News, Disinformation and Conspiracy Theories.* San Francisco: Chronicle Books, 2022.

Thompson, V. C. *The Earth Is Flat.* Ann Arbor, MI: Cherry Lake Publishing, 2023.

Internet Sites

10 Ways You Can Tell the Earth Is Round

popsci.com/10-ways-you-can-prove-earth-is-round/

Active Wild: Megalodon Facts

activewild.com/megalodon-facts/

BBC: Chemtrails: What's the Truth Behind the Conspiracy Theory?

bbc.com/news/blogs-trending-62240071

Index

airplanes, 4, 5, 9, 10
Antarctica, 9, 10
atmosphere, 5

birds, 14, 15, 16, 17

Central Intelligence Agency (CIA), 15
chemtrails, 4, 5
contrails, 4, 5

drones, 14, 15, 16

earthquakes, 25
eclipses, 13

flat-earthers, 8, 9
fossils, 20

government, 4, 6, 14, 15, 23
gravity, 9, 10, 11, 25, 26

Halley, Edmond, 23

magnetic fields, 23, 26
megalodons, 18, 19, 20, 21

poles, 13, 23, 24

research, 7, 10, 28, 29
robots, 14, 15, 17

satellites, 24
shadows, 13
shells, 22, 23
stars, 12, 13, 26

teeth, 20, 21

About the Author

Dr. Phill Simpson is an award-winning author of many novels, chapter books, and other books for children. He has also written more than 100 books for the global education market.

When he's not writing, he works as an elementary school teacher and educational consultant. Phill lives and writes in Auckland, New Zealand, with his wife Rose, their son, Jack, and their two border terriers, Whiskey and Raffles.